GRRRANIMALS:

Unforgettable Land and Water Creatures

I0157489

Story by Dr. Phineas Peabody
Illustrations by Steve McGinnis

PEABODY PUBLISHING COMPANY
Colorado Springs, Colorado, USA

GRRRANIMALS: Unforgettable Land and Water Creatures
By Dr. Phineas Peabody
Illustrations by Steve McGinnis

To my wife (Becky) – who continues to support all my dreams
—Phineas Peabody

To all the creative creatures in my mind, may you never leave me alone
—Steve McGinnis

Peabody Publishing Co., LLC
325 Thames Drive
Colorado Springs, CO 80906

Hardcover ISBN: 978-0-9963323-9-2
Paperback ISBN: 978-0-9963323-8-5
Also available in Kindle ebook format

Library of Congress Control Number: 2015942193

Peabody Publishing – *"Where we experience the wonder of a child."*

Become part of our journey at www.drphineaspeabody.com

DEDICATION

To Riley and Gabby - our loving and adorable pooches.

For all the joy they bring and all the chaos.
For their love and excitement to experience nature.
For their love of all creatures – both human and animal.
"May they live to be a thousand years old – in doggy years."

Antoine the *Angry* Alligator –
    has been around for eons of time.

He sports a long tail and snout –
    and lots of big teeth that shine.

He can swim underwater like a fish –
    or simply bask on the bank and waste time;

But you better watch out! Be careful!
    You know Antoine is not very kind.

Bevonshire the *Busy* Beaver –
> his friends call him '*Bevo*' for short;

He thrives in lakes, streams and rivers –
> where he builds the family's fort.

Bevo's naturally a busy beaver –
> but sometimes he just likes to be *l-a-z-y!*

Living with his clan on the water –
> where life is wet and wild and *c-r-a-z-y!*

Chester the *Channel* Catfish –
   has soft whiskers like a cat;
He hides in river bottoms –
   where he eats and gets real fat.
He has beady, shark-like eyes –
   and sharp fins that stick and prick;
With one stab of his pointed fin –
   his venom can make you feel sick!

Didi the *Darling* **Dragonfly** –
  can't swim or crawl or hop or bite.

She soars above lakes and ponds –
  where she zips about in flight.

Her tiny wings flutter with ease –
  as she is ever on the go…

Didi's not a real flashy sort –
  but she puts on a dazzling show!

Elvira the *Electric* Eel –
    might jolt you with electric shocks.
If you stray too close to her home –
    where she's hiding among the rocks.
Elvira is sly and sneaky –
    just like a reptilian snake.
And she'll give you a zap for sure –
    if you don't stay wide-eyed awake!

Freeda the *Frolicking* Frog –
   one of nature's loving creatures;
She's nimble on land and in water –
   and she has many striking features.

She hops and hops and hops around –
   and does so with elegant ease;
And when Freeda B-U-R-P-S out loud –
   it's the loudest we all agree.

Georgianna the *Gnagging* Gnat –
   is the peskiest pest around.

She'll bug you for hours and hours –
   while hardly making a sound.

Georgie is small in size and stature –
   still, she proves to be one giant pest;

When she targets the human species –
   she does so with a diligent zest.

Hugo the *Humongous* **Hippo** –
　　Wow! He must weigh a ton times two!

If he ever starts running towards you;
　　my advice is: "you better run too!"

Hugo looks quite large and awkward –
　　while he's out and about on land –

But when he steps in the water –
　　no other beast seems quite as grand.

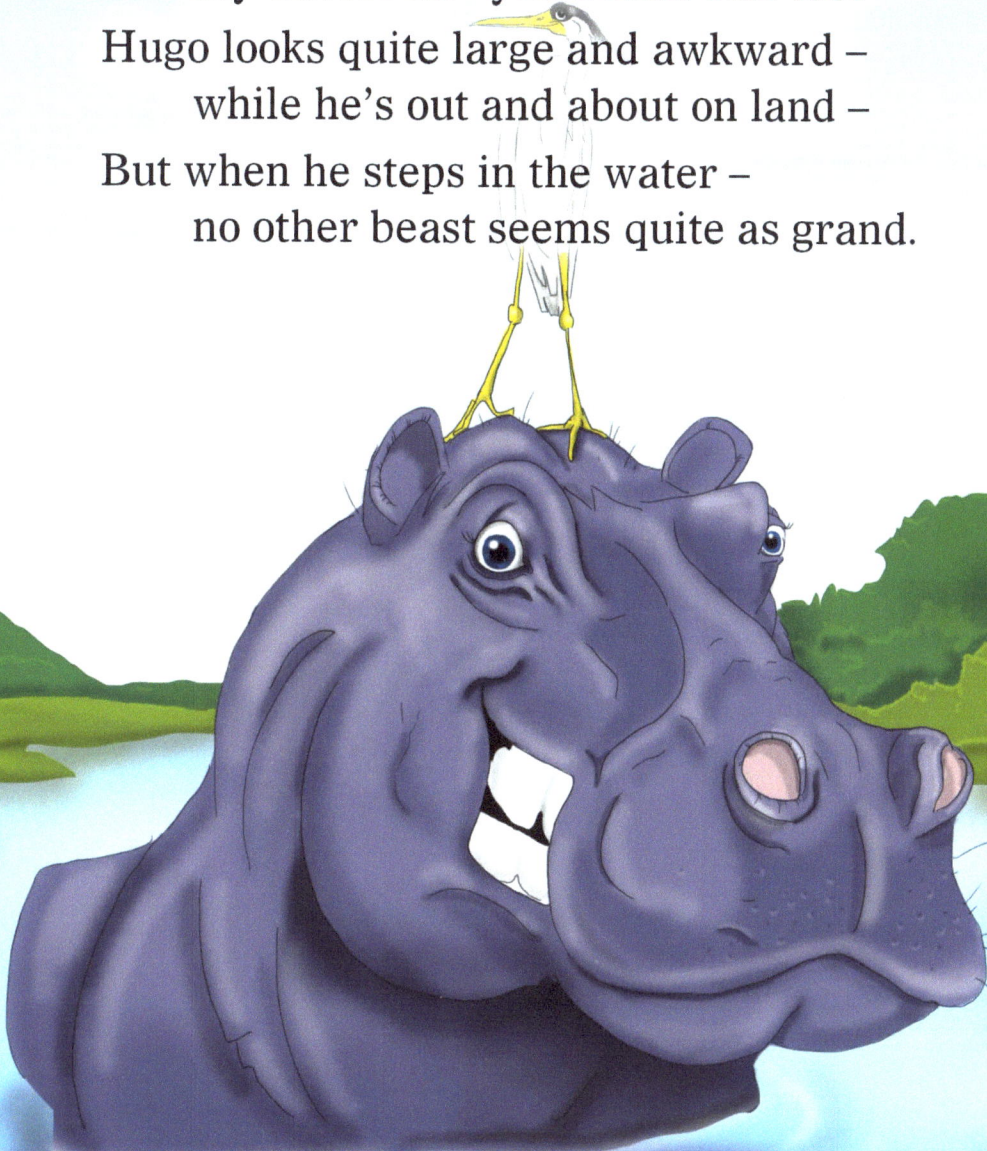

Icky the *Incredible* Ink Fish –
spends his life in the deep ocean blue.

He's not like those other fish in the sea.
He's a cephalopod – now here's a clue.

Whenever a big bully comes near him –
and tries to put Icky on the buffet;

Icky smiles and enjoys the last laugh –
then blasts them with his famous *ink* spray!

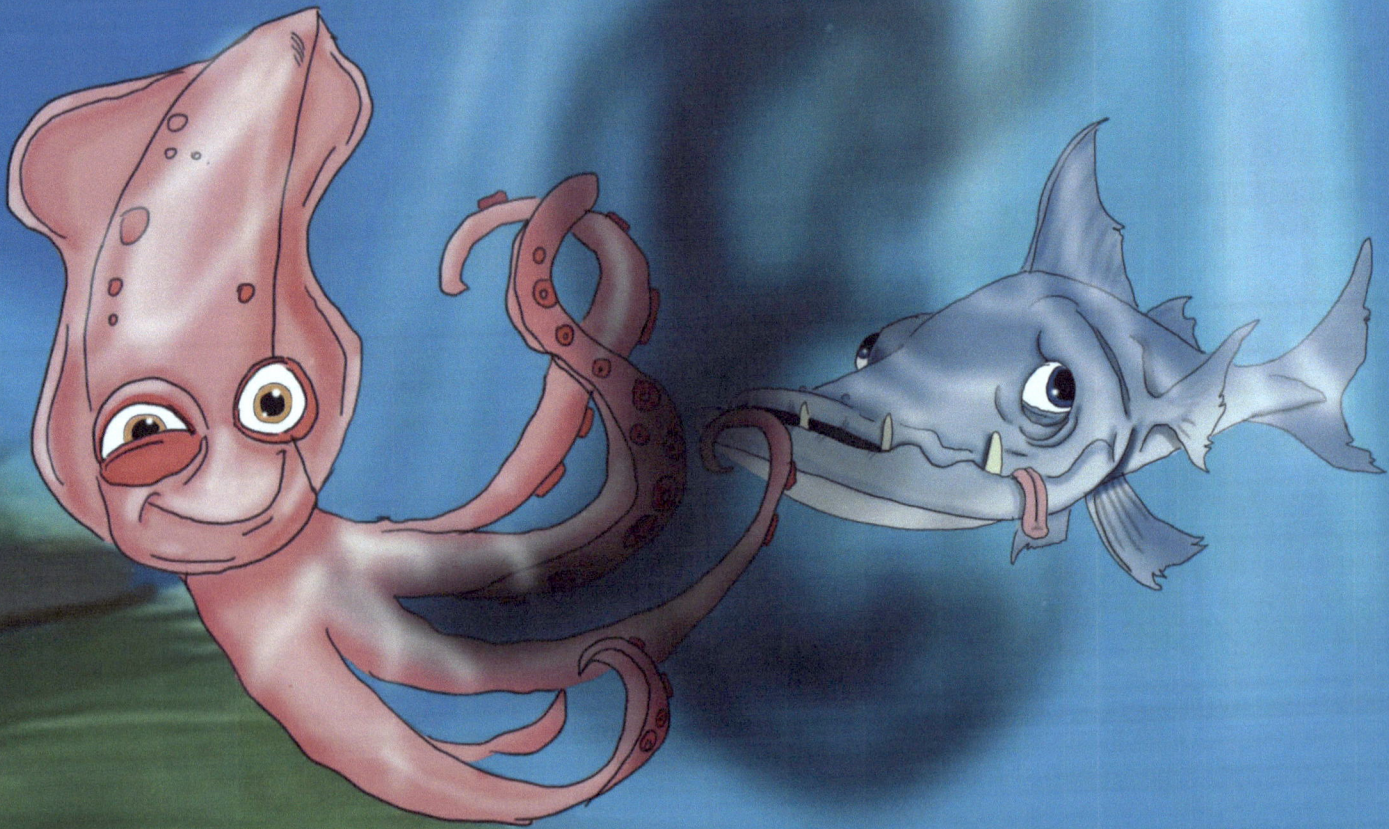

Jasper the *Jumbo* Box Jellyfish –
   a strange sight in our oceans and seas;

His head is shaped like an umbrella –
   and he has long arms that sting like bees.

Jasper glides about in the ocean –
   bobbing up and down and side to side;

He's been around for millions of years –
   at the mercy of the ocean's tide.

Kramer the Giant *Killer* Whale –
    is called *Orca* by friends and foes.
He's king in all the world's oceans –
    in both the North and the South poles.

Kramer is a black and white mammal –
    and his skin is very soft to feel;
He swims up to thirty miles an hour –
    and his favorite food is the *seal*.

Lydia the *Lady* Sea Lion –
    loves to swim and play and have fun;

She travels the seas to safe harbors –
    to eat and bask in the noon-day sun.

She can swim with ease under water –
    or use her flippers to walk on land;

Lydia also lives in city zoos –
    performing for all who'll give her a hand.

Milo the *Massive* **Manatee** –
    is a famous ocean *Sea Cow*;

He's a giant marine mammal –
    with a sad-looking wrinkled brow!

Milo prefers much warmer waters –
    like Florida and the Caribbean;

And if you ever see him up close –
    you might ask: "What is this I'm seein'?"

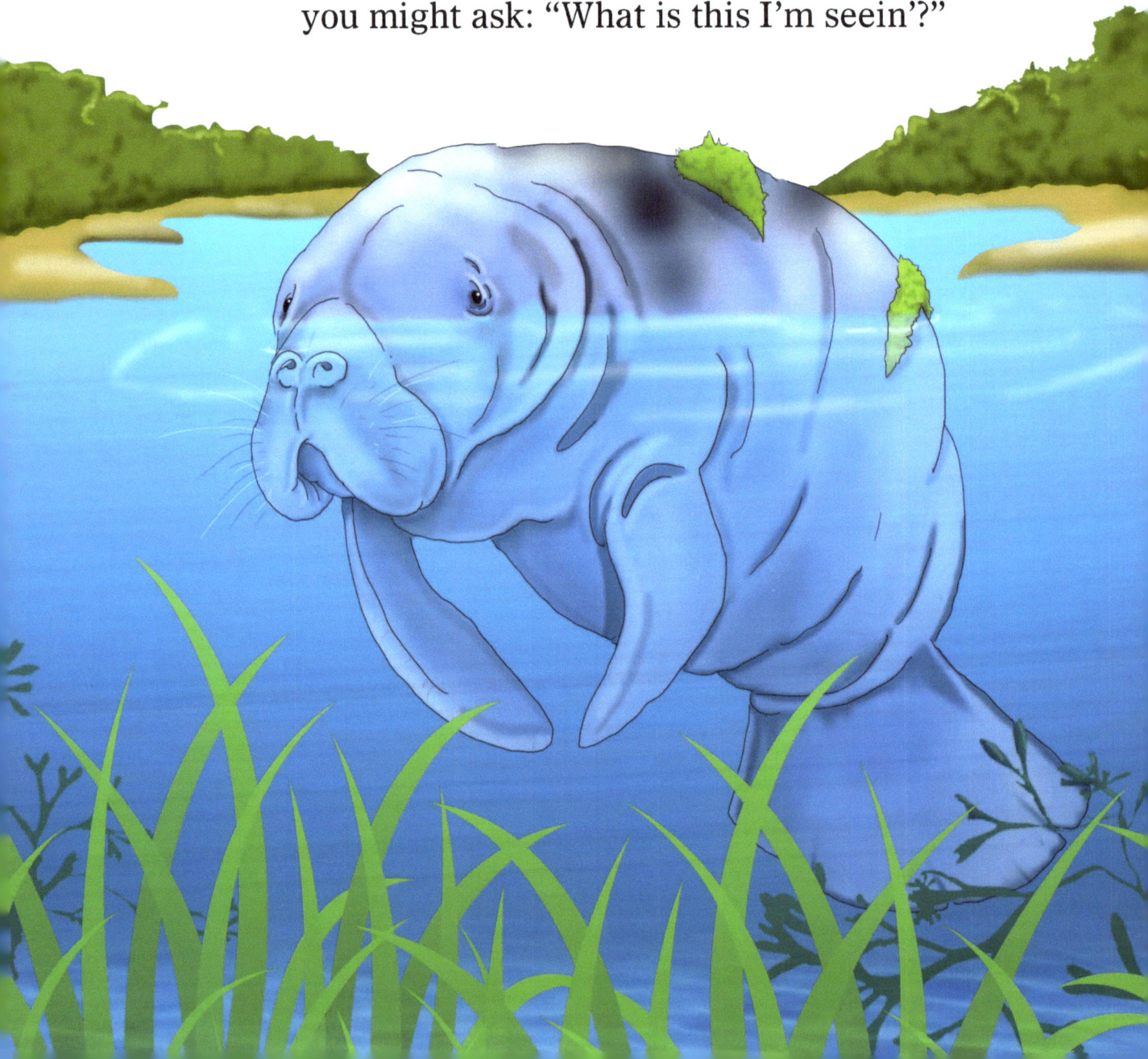

Nathan the *Nifty* Nutria –
   looks like a giant river *rat*.

He's a clever web-footed rodent –
   perhaps kin to the common *muskrat*.

Nate likes to snuggle in burrows –
   close to a freshwater supply;

He's a scary looking creature on land –
   I'm just glad he doesn't know how to fly.

Opal the *Obnoxious* Octopus –
  has a creepy head joined to eight arms;

Her looks appear strangely disturbing –
  and her presence sounds all the alarms.

She has three hearts for pumping blood –
  and two round piercing watchful eyes;

Opal has no skeletal system –
  but she's no doubt – the queen of disguise!

Percy the *Persnickety* **Pelican** –
   is a monstrous bird and menacing sight.

He has a mammoth nine-foot wing span –
   that helps keep Persnickety in flight.

His extra-large beak acts like a shovel –
   with a secret pouch for scooping up fish;

And when he swoops down on his prey –
   all you will hear is Swish! Swish! Swish!

Queenie the *Quintessential* Quail –
    a peaceful bird – and wee in size;
She nests in tall grass and hidden hollows –
    and seldom if ever soars to the skies.

Except when she might fear for her life –
    she attempts flight to flee from her foes.
Queenie is a quaint and charming fowl –
    or so I suppose her story goes.

Roscoe the *Raging* **Rhinoceros** –
    is simply known to all as 'R-h-i-n-o.'

Most rhinos are brown or gray or black –
    but some rhinos can be *a-l-b-i-n-o*.

Roscoe lives in Africa and Asia –
    the second largest beast on the planet;

He has a huge horn above his nose –
    and his skin is as thick as granite.

Sabrina the *Salty* Seahorse –
    spends her life bobbing up and down.
She can change her colorful colors –
    to camouflage when dangers abound.
She uses her snout to take in food –
    and a long tail to anchor her down;
Sabrina is an endangered species –
    and so one day, she might cease to be found.

Theodore the *Tiger* Shark –
 the "striped tiger" of the sea.
He's the fourth largest shark in the ocean –
 one of many you might see in the sea.
Teddy prowls day and night for food –
 for turtles, birds, fish and for seal;
He's a major force in nature for sure –
 an apex predator – he's the real deal!

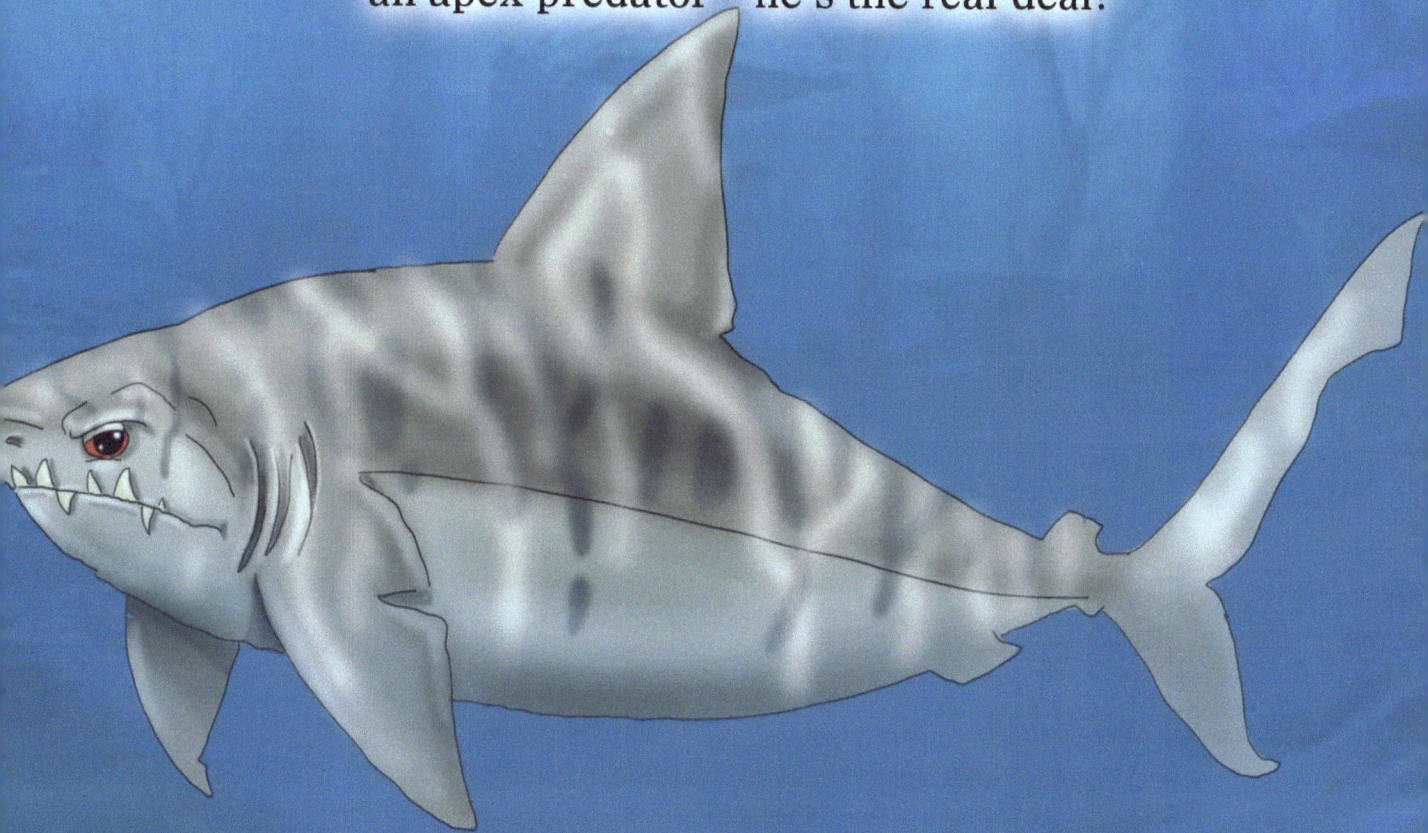

Ulysses the *Unique* Uakari –
    lives in the Amazon high in the trees;
Swinging from limb to limb to limb –
    and enjoying the gentle breeze.

This monkey is one of a kind –
    his bald face is brilliant bright red.
You'll find Ulysses in the jungle –
    in the rainforest – high overhead.

Valentino the *Venomous* **Viper** –
   lives everywhere but the Arctic Circle.

He can be green or brown or black –
   most any color but purple.

His fangs are prolonged and scary –
   his eyes seek out the unwary.

So, watch out for him my bambino –
   read about him in your library.

Winona the *Wary* Wildebeest –
  is quite shy and a bit worrisome.

In trying to flee from all her captors –
  all her efforts do become wearisome.

Winona looks like a wild bull –
  with sharp horns and vigilant eyes;

But she's afraid of her own shadow –
  if she sees it, she lays down and cries.

Xavier the *X-Ray* Tetra –
    a small – schooling kind of fish.
He lives in the Amazon River –
    it's here that he truly does flourish.

Xavier is quite shy and passive –
    not like those fish called piranhas;
Tetras spend their life in the river –
    it's their home – much like the savannas.

Yancy the *Yakkity* Yak –
      looks like a water buffalo.

He lives high in the Himalayas –
      where he grazes with mucho gusto.

Yancy travels most often in large herds –
      keeping tabs with other yakkity yaks;

He uses his horns for protection –
      from those predators that travel in packs.

Zoey the *Zany* Zonkey –
   is a bizarre sight to *s-e-e*;
She's a rare hybrid species –
   half zebra and half *d-o-n-k-e-y*.

If mom's a zebra and dad's a donkey –
   then a Zedonk this Zonkey would be.
I'm getting more and more confused you see –
   is Zoey a Zedonk or a Zonkey?

www.ingramcontent.com/pod-product-compliance
Lightning Source LLC
Chambersburg PA
CBHW042109040426
42448CB00002B/194